LEADER'S GUIDE

Gotta Have It!

It's a Stewardship Thing

CRC Publications
Grand Rapids, Michigan

ACKNOWLEDGMENTS

CRC Publications is grateful to Robert De Vries, professor of church education at Calvin Theological Seminary, Grand Rapids, Michigan, and the members of his curriculum development and design class for their contributions to the development of this course.

The Scripture quotations in this publication are from the HOLY BIBLE, NEW INTERNATIONAL VERSION, © 1973, 1978, 1984, International Bible Society. Used by permission of Zondervan Bible Publishers.

Gotta Have It!
It's a Stewardship Thing

LifeWise
© 1995 CRC Publications
2850 Kalamazoo Ave. SE
Grand Rapids, Michigan 49560

ISBN 1-56212-084-0

9 8 7 6 5 4 3 2

Contents

Preface

This study booklet was written by members of our class at Calvin Theological Seminary as a project to learn curriculum development and design. In a period of nine short weeks we plunged into the project, pulled together many resources, and finally wrote the four meeting plans in this leader's guide.

We recognize that most individuals, regardless of age, who live within North American culture are increasingly pressured with the lure of "things": this course is intended to give teens an opportunity to express the spiritual side of stewardship.

We know that many of the young people who will use these materials have their values in the right place. We want to affirm them in that. We also want to assure them that even though making hard choices about material things is tough sometimes, God will honor and bless them. Gaining a Christian perspective on material things early in life is one of the most critical tasks teens can accomplish.

We offer this material with the prayer that the young people who use it will know that every good and perfect thing comes from our Father in heaven, and that we can live a life of joy and pleasure with what he gives us.

Randy Buist
Debra Hitziger
Monica Hwang
Jonatan Palomino
Angel Rodriguez
Regina Smith

Martin Tel
Susan Vander Laan
Kenneth Vanderploeg
Suzanne Van Engen
Robert De Vries, teacher

Introduction

Life for today's young people is increasingly complex and confusing. Through this series, we want to help high school age young people find a basic frame of reference for living in this sometimes difficult world. By inviting teens to openly and actively express their faith, both in word and in deed, we can help them become a positive force for change in their complex world of work, school, and society.

Our goals for this series are as follows:

- to promote a healthy discussion of life issues
- to develop a biblical and Reformed perspective on life issues
- to make choices that are rooted in God's Word
- to grow in our personal commitment to live as God's people in a secular culture

Gotta Have It! is part of the LifeWise series for high school youth. Each course in the series offers four sessions dedicated to issues that are important to young people. The courses include a complete leader's guide with step-by-step instructions for leading group meetings and a book of perforated handouts.

These courses are intended to create a forum for discussion of important issues. You, as group leader, will be facilitating that discussion as together your group addresses different problems. You will encourage group members to think critically about where they stand personally in relation to these issues, and how that stance affects the way they act and live on a day-to-day basis.

THEME OF "GOTTA HAVE IT"

This course is designed to help participants develop a perspective on the materialistic culture in which we live. It will help us see how the rampant push for possessions affects us every day, and how our lifestyle choices

and practices can reflect our Christian commitment. Following is a brief outline of the course contents:

- Meeting 1 focuses on the difference between needs and wants. It establishes a biblical basis for stewardship by comparing our own attitudes with those of young King Solomon, who requested wisdom, not wealth.
- Meetings 2 and 3 apply the principles discussed in the first meeting to specific situations—money and physical appearance.
- Meeting 4 uses the parable of the talents to help us think about how we're using our God-given resources to further the cause of Christ in the world. This session also reviews the course and invites individuals to set specific goals.

MATERIALS

To lead the course you'll need this leader's guide and a book of handouts for yourself and one for each group member. The leader's guide and handouts are explained in more detail below.

You'll also need Bibles, paper and pencils or pens, markers, and a pad of newsprint or other large sheets of paper. Check the *Materials* list of each meeting for any other items needed to lead the session.

AUDIENCE AND GENERAL APPROACH

This course is designed for four discussion-based meetings and is intended for use by high school age youth. It can be used in church school, youth group, or retreat settings.

Ideally, you should have a full hour for each of the four meetings. You'll find there are plenty of activities to fill sixty minutes or more. Should you have less time, you'll need to trim or even omit some suggested steps. In any event, don't settle for less than forty-five minutes per meeting.

This course uses many group activities. They're lively and fun, and they help participants learn from each other. They are designed to encourage participants to delve into each issue, to think deeply about how each issue affects their lives, and to discuss each issue from a Christian perspective.

LEADER'S ROLE

As leader, your main tasks are the following:

- to get to know each group member
- to keep the various activities moving and on track
- to facilitate discussion and interaction
- to model what it means to be open to God's Word and Spirit

Try to cultivate an atmosphere of openness with the group that allows each person to feel free and secure. Think of yourself as a co-learner with the group, a fellow traveler on a journey of faith.

To prepare for each meeting, carefully read through the leader's guide material. This material is explained for you below.

USING THE LEADER'S GUIDE

This leader's guide will help you prepare for and lead the meetings. It will tell you when and how to use the handouts that accompany this course.

Today's Theme
This brief introductory section is intended to start you thinking about the day's theme and what the issue at hand means for the kids in your group.

Goals of the Meeting
Each meeting plan provides a set of goals that you can refer to throughout your meeting time to keep your discussion on track. These goals should constitute a guideline for your meeting, not a strict rule. We encourage you to add or modify goals as needed to fit the needs and interests of the teens in your group.

Materials
This section lists all the materials you'll need for the meeting, including any materials you'll need for warm-up group activities.

Theme Thoughts
This section is designed to give you, as leader, a deeper biblical/theological perspective on the issue you're addressing in the meeting. Please resist any impulse to lecture to the group on this section's contents. It's just for you.

Meeting Plan (Steps)
Different every meeting, these steps are designed to give you interesting and "active" methods for reaching the goals of the meeting. Some of these steps use the handouts, others do not.

Options
These optional activities are intended to increase your flexibility in leading your group and to stimulate your creativity. Substitute these steps for others in the meeting plan when and if you feel that the option would be more meaningful or appealing to your group members.

Handouts
You should order a book of perforated handouts for each group member and for yourself. Prior to each meeting time, tear the necessary handouts from each book and have them ready to distribute at the appropriate time.

The handouts are used from time to time for a variety of activities. They contain prompts for biblical study, case studies, group activities, reprinted articles that deal with the issue to be discussed, and, occasionally, optional activities for following up the group's discussion at home. Handouts are numbered sequentially throughout the course.

ADDITIONAL SUGGESTIONS FOR LEADERS

Be personal!
First, be personal in the sense of being yourself. Don't try to be something you normally aren't. Most teens can immediately see through an adult who is trying to be "cool" just to impress them. Be yourself, and act your age.

Second, be personal in the sense that you respect each young person for who he or she is, for the strength of his or her character, and for his or her ability to reason and apply what he or she is learning through these meetings.

Third, be personal in the way you see yourself: as a leader but also as a colearner with the group. Let them know you don't have all the answers, that you are on a faith journey *with* them.

Don't be afraid to say "I don't know" or "I'm not sure" or "Help me think that through, will you?" Applying our Christian principles to issues can be difficult and perplexing—for adults as well as for young people.

Be a good listener
Resist the temptation to do all of the talking yourself (otherwise known as lecturing). Learn to be a good listener, even if it means patiently enduring times of silence. Give group members time to think and to respond. Show by your comments and your body language that you appreciate their contributions (even if you don't agree with everything they say).

When you do ask questions, remember to keep a good balance of questions of *fact,* questions of *opinion* or interpretation, and questions of *foundations.* The last category of questions asks people to explain the basis on which they have made their judgments. An important part of your task is to help your group recognize the value of basing their judgments on Scripture and on the teachings of the church.

Look for and take advantage of opportunities for your group members to take responsibility for the meeting's activities. In doing so you'll provide them with a sense of ownership for the group discussion and activities.

Be creative
Use this material to guide—not dictate—your discussion. Adapting the discussion topics and activities to better suit your situation should be your goal as a group leader. We offer several alternative steps at the end of each meeting plan to allow you more flexibility and choice in leading your meetings.

You may find that each meeting has more material in it than you can cover in the time you have available. Feel free to pick and choose between the steps, the options at the end of the meeting plan, and your own ideas. Make it *your* meeting, tailored to the needs and interests of *your* group.

Have fun!
Learning is meant to be enjoyable. God calls us to enjoy him and to celebrate his goodness. Reflect that celebration in your setting. If you are confined to a room at church, avoid placing the chairs in an arrangement that looks and feels like school. Use the games and other exercises not only to learn together but also to laugh together.

EVALUATION FORMS

At the end of this manual is a leader's evaluation form for you to complete. An evaluation form for group members is included in the handouts for this course. You can help us improve this series by completing these forms.

Please send completed evaluation forms to:

LifeWise
CRC Publications
2850 Kalamazoo Ave. SE
Grand Rapids, Michigan 49560

If you prefer, call us at 1-800-333-8300 or e-mail your comments to editors@crcpublications.org.

"I Want It, So I *Must* Need It"

TODAY'S THEME

Ever since they were little children, the young people in your group have been trying to figure out what they *want*. More than likely, they can remember being asked, "So—what do you want for your birthday?"

Now that they're older, their wants are becoming increasingly complex and urgent. As their friends acquire more and more possessions, the pressure to keep up is just that much more intense. And they're looking for more big-ticket items now, too: designer clothing, the latest computer, the right music (and the equipment to play it on), even a set of their own wheels.

In the midst of trying to figure out what we *want,* we in our North American society have often lost sight of what we really *need*. This meeting discusses the differences between what we *want* and what we, especially as God's people, *need* to live a full life in Christ.

GOALS OF THE MEETING

- to list ten important possessions and classify them as needs or wants
- to describe Solomon's ability to distinguish his needs from his wants
- to compare Solomon's needs and wants with our own
- to ask God to show us what's truly important in our lives

MATERIALS

1. Bibles
2. Pencils and paper
3. Chalkboard or newsprint
4. Handouts 1-3
5. $5,000 in play money for each group member (see step 1)
6. 15 lunch bags to hold the items to be "purchased"

THEME THOUGHTS

The pull between our needs and wants is one we all share. By *needs* we mean whatever is necessary to serve God's kingdom. By *wants* we mean those things we yearn for to satisfy our own desires. Our culture's priorities are at odds with what our priorities should be as God's people. These priorities can easily cloud our perceptions so that we stop depending on God to satisfy our needs.

God has always provided for his people's needs—recall the stories of water and manna in the wilderness (Ex. 15-17) and Elijah's involvement with the oil and the flour that never ran out (1 Kings 17). Jesus tells his disciples that they are not to worry about what they will eat, drink, or wear (Matt. 6:25-34), because God will take care of those needs. Faithful followers of Christ should seek the kingdom of God rather than their own needs, fully confident that their needs will be met.

During this meeting, you and your group members will consider the story of Solomon. After his father, David, died and Solomon assumed the throne of Israel, he realized what an awesome task lay ahead of him. Although twenty-year-old Solomon could have asked God for anything he wanted, he asked for "a discerning heart to govern your people and to distinguish between right and wrong" (1 Kings 3:9). Solomon knew he would need these qualities more than anything else so that he could rule Israel properly. He knew the difference between his *wants* (riches, power) and his *needs* (wisdom to rule properly). He trusted that God would provide everything he needed. And God blessed Solomon for having that trust.

The problem of discerning between wants and needs is not limited to teenagers. As a discussion leader, you have an opportunity during your meeting to model for your teens the decisions you have had to make in your own life between wants and needs. Tell them about a time when you chose to satisfy your wants rather than your needs, and what lessons you learned from that experience. Also tell them about a time when you chose the right way and how God blessed you in that decision. Honestly discussing your own difficulty with materialism will impress on the teens in your group the importance of setting the right priorities. And it will allow them to see you as one who struggles right along with them.

It's a struggle that we all deal with every day. We live in a society that literally screams at us through the media that we've "gotta have it!" Everything from athletic shoes to automobiles, hamburgers to hair-care products, soda to sound systems are all packaged under slogans telling us that the image we project is more important than who we are. A long-running hair coloring ad proclaims, "I indulge myself because I'm worth it," blatantly setting the standard for a self-oriented consumer society. The daily barrage of advertising that pummels you and the kids in your group— from radio, television, billboards, and print media—amounts to a powerful force that shapes what we think, say, and do.

But that's not all—consumer-based North American cultural biases are also omnipresent in the music we listen to and the television shows and movies that we watch. These forms of entertainment—so important in defining our culture—create a model of materialism that today's young people struggle to emulate.

Throughout this meeting, invite your teens to look at Solomon's choice. As you do the activities together, work with the kids to look at yourselves in comparison to Solomon. And be assured that God's faithfulness continues to all who set kingdom priorities ahead of their own personal priorities.

For Further Study
The Bible is packed with passages that deal with greed, money, and satisfaction. Check out the following passages as background for this meeting's discussion:

Proverbs 17:16
Matthew 6:8-13
Mark 10:17-25
Luke 12:15-34
Philippians 4:4-19
James 2:5
1 John 3:17

MEETING PLAN

1 "WHAT'S IT WORTH?"
15-20 minutes

Write one of the phrases printed below on the outside of each paper bag you've brought to today's session. Inside each bag, place several slips of paper with the same phrase printed on them (if you have a large group, limit the number of slips in each bag to one-third of the total number of group members):

- a long life free of illness
- a group of close friends
- to live in an unspoiled natural setting
- a satisfying love relationship
- an opportunity to eliminate human suffering
- a great-looking car that will never rust or break down
- power to influence the world's leaders
- a happy family relationship
- unlimited meals in any of the world's restaurants
- the ability to preserve endangered species
- a reputation as a wise decision maker
- a world without war
- an unlimited supply of the latest clothes and accessories
- elimination of air and water pollution
- a lifetime movie pass

Directions:

- Give each group member a pencil and $5,000 in play money.
- Each person must "shop" around the table once or twice before they buy anything.
- Each person must spend all of his or her money, and should pay the most for the things that are most valuable to him or her.
- Group members must circle the table on which the bags are displayed, "buying" available slips by putting the amount of money in the bag that they are willing to pay for that item.
- Participants must mark on each slip they buy the amount of money they paid for that item.
- Once all the slips have been bought, kids can barter with each other should they wish to trade items with other people.

After the buying and trading have been completed, ask each person to take a bag or two and count the money that's inside it. As they tell the amounts they've counted, you can write the categories and amounts on your chalkboard (or on newsprint). When your list is complete, go back through it and note the rank of each item (that is, which item was most wanted, which second most wanted, and so on).

Hold a brief discussion so that everyone can give a brief explanation of why they made their particular selections. Let them draw some tentative conclusions about the kinds of things we value the most.

2 TAKING INVENTORY— A PERSONAL ACTIVITY
15 minutes

This exercise is similar to the previous one, but it involves group members personally rather than focusing on the items in the bags.

Give each participant a piece of paper and a pencil, and ask them to take an inventory of the ten possessions that are most important to

them personally. Have them rank these possessions from 1 (most important) to 10 (least important).

Once they have made their lists, they should mark each item as something they *need* or something they *want*. Since this is a private inventory, the kids should be allowed to keep their lists to themselves if they want to. However, if they want to discuss possessions and priorities with their peers, encourage them in that direction by asking them to form small discussion groups of three to four persons each.

Whether they choose to discuss their findings or keep them private, ask the kids to take their inventories home for use in their personal reflection during the week.

---

3 GROUP DISCUSSION
15 minutes

Distribute Handout 1 ("Reader's Theater") to each group member (tear the handouts from the perforated book prior to today's meeting). Using Handout 1, read the story of King Solomon (1 Kings 3:5-15) as a group. The reader's theater format will encourage kids to put themselves in Solomon's place—to really evaluate how he thought and what he felt at the time. Ask for volunteers to read the parts of narrator, Solomon, and God. The rest of the group can spontaneously chime in with some of "Solomon's thoughts" as he makes his decision.

Then look together at the questions at the end of Handout 1. Guidelines for your discussion follow:

1. How do you think Solomon felt when the Lord appeared to him in a dream?
Was Solomon surprised to receive a visit from God? Scripture doesn't mention any such shock or surprise. Apparently Solomon was quite preoccupied with his new responsibilities in the days preceding the dream. So when God came to him, Solomon didn't hesitate to

pour out his heart. He thanked God for the grace shown both to himself and to his father, David, and told God about the anxiety he had about ruling Israel. He must have, however, been amazed by God's generous offer to "ask for whatever you want me to give you."

2. Imagine yourself in Solomon's place: a twenty-year-old king who had absolute power over millions of people, a king for whom God had just written a blank check ("Ask for whatever you want me to give you"). If you were in Solomon's place, what might you have been tempted to ask for?

Listen to the various suggestions, then note that God himself outlined some of the requests that were typical of Solomon's royal contemporaries: a long life, great wealth, and revenge on personal and political enemies. None of these were on Solomon's mind when he spoke to God in his dream.

3. How does this passage show Solomon's ability to distinguish between wants and needs?

Faced with the offer of receiving anything in the world that he wanted, Solomon chose the one thing that he truly needed: wisdom from God in leading the people of Israel. He didn't even consider asking for anything else.

4. Why would Solomon ask God for something like "wisdom" when he could have received fabulous wealth and power?

Solomon realized that he had great need for wisdom. God had given the young king awesome responsibilities. Today's leaders have large legislative systems to help them make decisions or to limit their power, but Solomon had no such backup. Certainly he had advisors, but as king his decisions were the last word. That's why he requested the aid of the ultimate political advisor, the one whom his father David had trusted and who had blessed David with a long and prosperous career. No doubt Solomon also trusted God to provide whatever else he needed in life.

5. In what ways are our own wants and needs similar to those of Solomon?

Solomon could have asked for virtually anything he wanted. All the wealth of the world was there to tempt him and, judging by his later lifestyle, such wealth no doubt did tempt him. If we're honest, we've got to admit that we too are tempted to go for all the toys and prestige our possession-crazy society can offer. And, like Solomon, we too need wisdom. You might explain that wisdom means more than just "street-smarts" or even good ethics. Wisdom is a way of looking at life that puts God in the center of things.

Please consider sharing some of your experiences with wants and needs. This would be a good time to tell the group about your struggles to resist the urge to always have more of the biggest and best and fastest items on the market. You might also mention a time when you placed kingdom priorities before your own, and how God blessed you in that decision.

---

4 APPLICATION ALERT!
10 minutes

To help your teens make this meeting's theme more personal, have them refer back to their private inventory lists (step 2). Ask them to review what they wrote there and consider the priority they put on certain items.

Then ask them to imagine the following scenario:

You have just been diagnosed with a terminal disease. Your doctor has told you that at most you have one month to live. As the reality of this news sets in, look again at your inventory list. How might you change your present list of "wants" and "needs"? What items would you switch around? What items might you add or delete?

Once group members have had time for private reflection, have them each write on an unsigned slip of paper the one most important thing—the thing they would *need* the most in this situation—on their list. Collect the slips, then write these items down on your chalkboard or newsprint. As a group, discuss the items that participants listed as their most important priority.

5 CLOSING

5 minutes

Before you close today's session, take a look at Handout 2 ("eVALUEation"). Encourage everyone to look over this brief handout, suggesting that it's like one of those "test yourself" quizzes in the magazines so many of your group members read. Ask them to take the handout home and to complete it as part of their reflection on today's session.

Using the final list that you made in step 4 as a guideline, lead the group in prayer, asking them to pray that God will show us what is truly most important in our lives. Provide some time for silent prayer and reflection as well. After a few moments, end the meeting by reading Philippians 4:8 and 19.

OPTIONS

HANDOUT 3 ("WHAT DO YOU OWN?")

If you have enough time during the session, distribute this optional handout at the beginning of step 2, asking kids to give it a quick reading before they make their personal lists of needs and wants. If you can't fit this handout into your session, save it and give it to the kids as they leave. Invite them to read it at home and think about where they personally might fit in the research.

SCRIPTURE STUDY

If you'd like to encourage more Bible study on the topic of "wants" and "needs," you could use the passages listed in For Further Study under the Theme Thoughts section (as well as Matt. 6:25-34) as a starting point for a discussion on what the Bible says about setting priorities. You might use this as a substitute for the activity in step 1.

SOLOMON'S STORY

If you feel you'll run short on time today, you could save a bit of time by reading through (or having a group member read through) Solomon's story from 1 Kings 3:5-15. Follow the reading either by asking the questions from the handout yourself or by writing them on newsprint or on a chalkboard.

HANDOUT 2 ("eVALUEation")

You might integrate this handout into the session by substituting it for the "What's It Worth?" activity in step 1. This exercise will allow you and the teens in your group to look at what you value and what your attitudes toward materialism are. Encourage everyone to keep score and to find out where they stand on the scale provided.

Money Matters

Young people and money—an odd match if there ever was one. Although some of the young people in your group may have wealthy and generous parents and others may have part-time jobs, most young people find themselves in the situation of never having enough money for the things they want to do.

At their age, the teens in your group need to begin supporting themselves—after all, they're not children anymore. But they're not quite ready to get full-time employment yet, either. High school and college diplomas are increasingly important in our society, and such educational pursuits usually keep young people and money apart.

For all of us, money is both a *want* and a *need*—to use two words from the last meeting. How much we want money and what we do with it is all part of this meeting's discussion.

GOALS OF THE MEETING

• to explain what several Bible passages say about our use of money and material possessions
• to consider our own spending patterns in the light of biblical directives
• to consider ways to make better use of our material possessions
• to realize that all material gifts come from God

MATERIALS

1. Bibles
2. Pencils and paper
3. Chalkboard or newsprint
4. Handouts 4-6
5. A bowl or cup and 25 pennies for each group member

6. Blindfolds
7. Masking tape
8. Pocket calculators (optional)

THEME THOUGHTS

The first meeting helped us recognize the difference between wants (self-centered desires) and needs (things we need to be faithful stewards of God). Now we will focus specifically on how Christian teens can use their money responsibly.

The title of this session says that you'll discuss money matters in your meeting today. But the title is appropriate in another sense— it says that money *does* matter. It is very important to all of us, especially to teens.

In a recent survey among young people in the Christian Reformed Church, 74 percent said they spend about $20 each month in restaurants and 59 percent said they spend about that much on entertainment and on clothing. At the same time, 78 percent of those young people said they contribute less than $10 each month to a charity or church.

We all use money. We all need money to live in our society. Gaining the proper perspective on the use of our money, however, can be an extremely difficult task. According to Scripture, we must become responsible stewards of *all* the material things (including money) that God gives us to use. But fiscal responsibility is a lifelong lesson that many adults have never learned, a fact to which the credit-card companies and packed bankruptcy-court dockets can attest.

Being responsible with our money means first recognizing where our money comes from. After we've done that we can work to determine a balance between what we *want* to spend our money on and what we *need* to spend at least some of our money on, all with a view toward living the Christian life.

As you prepare to lead the teens in your group in a discussion about money, keep the following thoughts in mind:

First, consider the ultimate source of our income. As Christians, we recognize that God is the creator and the owner of all things (Gen. 1). And everything we have is a gift from God. God explicitly claims ownership of our money: "The silver is mine and the gold is mine" (Hag. 2:8). So the money we have in our wallets, purses, and pockets is not ours—it belongs to God. Since we're part of God's creation, we can't claim ownership of anything on this earth.

Some of the teens in your group may object to this idea. After all, don't we work hard to earn the money we have? Deuteronomy 8:18 sheds light on that subject when it says that God blesses us with the *ability* to earn money. Our talents and abilities and good day-to-day health are part of the gift of honest financial gain that God gives to us. So we should never boast about our ability to turn a profit. We should rather recognize that God, who is the source of our strength, provides us with the benefits of our work.

Second, the Bible establishes the principle that we must return to God a portion of all that we have. Whether we do it through a strict process of tithing (as suggested in the Old Testament) or follow the New Testament principle of laying aside our gifts to God every week, we must give our gifts as an act of gratitude toward God. 2 Corinthians 9:12-13 demonstrates how our faithful giving brings glory to God, and how in giving we become part of God's process of providing for others.

As part of providing for our daily care, God has created everything around us for our use. Many of God's material gifts are wonderful and fill us with joy and happiness. But material things must never blind us to the source of true joy—our Lord Jesus Christ.

The hope that we have in our Savior is infinitely more precious than any amount of this world's money, however pleasant or useful that money might be.

Challenge your teens in this meeting to see and discuss the fact that "a man's life does not consist in the abundance of his possessions" (Luke 12:15), but that our worth depends on our relationship to Jesus Christ. Help them to concentrate on developing good stewardship practices rather than following the lure of money. Money only matters if it is put to work in the service of Christ and his kingdom.

For Further Study
If you have more time to dig into Scripture, check out some of these classic passages from the Old Testament:

Deuteronomy 14:22-23
1 Chronicles 29:12
Psalm 39:6-7
Psalm 62:10
Proverbs 11:4, 28
Ecclesiastes 5:10

MEETING PLAN
_____

1 "MONEY MATTERS" GAME
10 minutes

To play the game, form as many teams as you can with at least two but no more than four members on each team. Have each team select a person to act as "coin catcher" and station him or her on one side of the room. Have the rest of the team members stand at least ten feet away from the coin catcher. Place a strip of masking tape on the floor or carpet. The team members aren't allowed to cross the tape (they'll be blindfolded so it's best if they keep their feet stationary!). Also place a strip of tape in front of the coin catcher.

Give each team member a bowl of 25 pennies. Give the coin catchers small paper cups.

If you have a large enough room, each team can play the game simultaneously. If your room is small, have the teams take turns.

Directions
- Team members will gently toss their pennies across the room toward their team's coin catcher.
- All team members, except the coin catcher, will be blindfolded.
- The coin catcher may only use one hand to hold the cup, and may only catch the coins in the cup. Any use of hands other than to hold the cup is not allowed.
- All pennies must be caught in the air. Any missed or spilled pennies must stay on the floor.
- Neither the coin catcher nor team members may cross the masking-tape barriers, but they can do anything else necessary to catch the pennies.
- The group leader will judge whether a tosser or a catcher has crossed the line. If anyone does cross, the team loses a penny from their cup.
- The winner of this game is the team who has the most pennies in their coin catcher's cup at the end of the game. The team that has the least amount of pennies in the cup has to clean up for the rest of the group.

When all the pennies have been tossed, find out which team won the game. Then have group members reflect on their experience by asking them to respond to the following questions:

1. How did you feel tossing pennies blind-folded?
2. If each penny were worth 100 dollars of your own money, would you have tossed them quite as easily?
3. What are some of the ways that we sometimes throw our money away as if we were blindfolded?

2 MONEY TALK
20 minutes

Divide your group into three teams and give a copy of Handout 4 to each group member. Ask them to read the instructions silently and then work together on the "Group Grapple" exercise. The purpose of this exercise is to help teens realize that they are responsible to God for all they have.

When each team has worked through their Scripture passages, give everyone time to think about the last question on their own. After a couple of minutes, reassemble the larger group and ask members of each team to report on what they discovered in the passages. If there are some who would like to volunteer their answer on the last question, welcome their responses.

3 BUDGET BREAKTHROUGH
20 minutes

Handout 5 ("Budget Breakthrough") contains a form that your teens can use to work on a personal budget. To introduce this activity, tell group members that in a world where consumerism runs rampant and so many things call for our attention, it's easy for us to get in over our heads by spending money on the things we *want* so that we don't have enough money for the things we *need*.

Some of the young people in your group may not see the usefulness in working on such a budget. Remind them of what we learned in the previous step: *all* that we have belongs to God—whether we have only a few bucks in our back pocket or a million-dollar trust fund stashed away. Budgets are necessary no matter what a person's income is.

First, review side 1 of Handout 5. Ask your group if they've ever felt like their money vanishes into thin air the minute they get it, and discuss the benefits of "keeping a leash" on their money.

This would be the perfect place to talk with the kids about your own experiences with money. Have you worked on your own personal budget? How do you set aside enough money to meet all your bills? Do you have a personal system that works for you? If so, share that system and your experiences with the group. Your example will go a long way toward meeting this session's goal of discovering the proper use of our money and resources.

Have several copies of the budget sheet available for each of your group members. As you work on personal budgets in your meeting today, tell the kids that they don't have to be exact in their figuring—for now, rough estimates will do nicely. When they take the other sheets home, they can be much more specific. If possible, have a few pocket calculators on hand for the kids to use as they do their figuring.

Encourage group members as they work on the form to be realistic and accurate when they allocate their resources. Tell them to consider how much they have been spending on each item. Also ask them to consider how they might have to adjust their spending patterns to cover their bills and to have the kind of money to purchase the things they'll need in the future: a car, new clothes, or a college education.

This may be the first time some of the kids in your group have been asked to categorize their spending patterns. Like many people, they may just spend until the money runs out. As they work on their budgets, impress upon the group that as they take on part-time jobs, begin to date, or look toward college, their needs will become greater. Their income will increase as well, but more money will do them no good unless they're able to handle it properly. Budgeting is a fact of life in the adult world. As such this activity is an extremely valuable tool.

It's important to note with the kids that this budget includes a category for church gifts and giving to other charitable organizations.

Charitable giving is a very important part of any budget-making exercise. As Christians, we give of the money that we have out of gratitude to God. Granted, there may be times when surprise expenses prohibit us from giving as much as we'd like. But the fact is, God doesn't need vast amounts of our money in order to work the miracle of generosity in our hearts. The privilege of giving to causes that support God's kingdom goes right along with God's gift to us of the ability to make money (see Theme Thoughts).

You may discover that there are several conscientious individuals in your group whose parents have taught them the benefits of budgeting and keeping track of their expenditures. If so, ask them to help others as they work, or to discuss with the group why they think keeping a budget is beneficial.

Once each person has developed a rough budget and determined how he or she might have to change personal spending patterns, talk for a few minutes about what this exercise has shown to them. Was it difficult to allocate their funds? Did they find any areas where they might want to change their spending habits? Is budgeting in this way a useful practice? Ask the kids to think of concrete ways that they can better use their money and their material possessions, and ask for volunteers to give some suggestions aloud.

---

4 CLOSING
5 minutes

Quickly review what you've learned together during this meeting about who owns the world and what our attitude as Christians ought to be toward our possessions. You can encourage everyone to take time to appraise their assets and really try sticking to the budget they made in this meeting. (*Note:* Place a stick-on note in your calendar to bring the budget issue up again in a month. At that time you can ask how group members are doing on keeping their budgets.)

Close by giving everyone a chance to say sentence prayers of thanks for God's gifts and requests for guidance in using them. The prayers can be silent or spoken. Go around the circle, giving each person an opportunity to pray. Ask people to say "Amen" after a silent prayer so that the next person knows when to begin.

As the kids leave your session today, remind them to finish working on their budget sheets during the week at home. Also give them a photocopy of Handout 6 ("Monte's Money Mishaps") for reading at home.

OPTIONS

SIT-DOWN SCAVENGER HUNT

You might want to substitute the following scavenger-hunt type activity for the penny-pitching game that begins today's session:

This activity is completed without leaving the room. The leader calls out a question, and anyone who has an item that fits the description should stand up to display or describe the item.

What do you have that you received from . . .

• a brother or sister?
• an aunt or uncle?
• a grandparent?
• a boyfriend or girlfriend?
• another friend?
• a teacher?
• your parents?
• God?

Notice that the first items will likely be material goods (clothes, money, pictures, etc.). Other possibilities might include love, friendship, education, and the like. Things received from parents could include hereditary characteristics such as looks, hair color, or height. Hopefully some of the kids will also respond with things less tangible such as security, personality, eternal life, forgiveness, acceptance. In the discussion, make certain

that your group members see that everything we have ultimately comes from God—even if others give it to us.

HANDOUT 6 ("MONTE'S MONEY MISHAPS")

This case study is a fictitious account of a young man's failure to plan for a major purchase. If you have time at the end of today's session, you may want to have kids read through the story and briefly discuss the questions at the end of the handout.

Looking Good!

What do you think? Are looks important to young people today or not?

Keep in mind while you're pondering this question that looking good is a matter of personal taste. A prom queen contestant in full battle gear might look good to most people—hair, makeup, dress, and accessories all coming together in one dazzling package. On the other hand, teenage hunk-watchers might swoon and squeal over the high school tough guy who's dressed in black boots, ripped jeans, and grungy flannels.

No doubt about it, personal appearance is a big item for kids. As Madison Avenue knows all too well, kids are willing to spend big bucks on looking good. A certain look identifies a person with other individuals or groups of people. Wearing heavy-metal rock band T-shirts and black makeup gives off a certain image; so does wearing clothes that come straight from the latest east coast catalog. By identifying themselves with a particular group, young people are trying to say something about themselves.

What they're saying can sometimes be dangerous. As teens strive for the perfect weight or the perfect body, they can damage their still-growing bodies. Eating disorders are not uncommon among teenage girls who try to emulate ultra-slim models. Some teenage boys put their future health in jeopardy by using steroids and other chemical substances to "bulk up."

All of this happens in our materialistic pursuit of the "right image." In this meeting we'll be challenged to evaluate the kind of image we aspire to and what that image conveys to others. We'll remind ourselves that when God commanded his people not to put any images before him, he also meant personal self-image.

As Christians, God calls us to love and serve him with all our being (heart, soul, strength, spirit, and body). One way to show our love for God is to have a healthy attitude about our personal appearance. This meeting will help us develop guidelines that apply to the physical (outward) side of our own personal walk with Christ.

- to discover how our personal appearance is (or should be) a window to our spiritual life
- to examine our decisions about personal appearance, contrasting North American materialistic values and God's values
- to evaluate our own appearance (outer as well as inner) to see how it honors or dishonors God
- to suggest Christian guidelines for personal appearance

1. Bibles
2. Pens/pencils
3. Handouts 7-10
4. Notecards
5. Scratch paper

You may be wondering what the topic of "looking good" has to do with materialism. There's a simple answer, of course: as a group, teens spend billions of dollars a year on personal-grooming products and clothing. The "gotta have it" attitude is very big when it comes to laying out cold cash for all the things advertisers claim make us "look good." On a deeper level too, kids' concern with appearances reflects our culture's preoccupation with the outward, the physical, the material.

You may find this session's task quite challenging. On the one hand, you want the kids in your group to think about what their personal appearance says. On the other hand, you don't want to start a shouting match or set off a competition between your group members for "looking good." Remember that a clean, well-kept appearance is not necessarily a sign of spiritual superiority. And some of our most-respected heroes of faith have dressed in odd ways—remember John the Baptist's camel-hair tuxedo?

Keep in mind that when speaking with teens about the topic of looking good, a certain amount of anxiety and difference of opinion is inevitable. As leader, be aware of your own personal views on appearance. Just as we rightly claim that we are culturally removed from the dress codes of the first century, so also the kids in your group may be culturally removed from your own standards. Fashion trends and hairstyles change from day to day, it seems. Many of your group members stand on the cutting edge of fashion and study the trends religiously. They may have strong feelings about the way they look and why. Keep an open mind!

Don't make the mistake of trying to convince your teens that we can totally ignore our cultural setting. Your group members will probably remind you that God has placed us all in a specific time and place. Diverse cultures and societies are a revelation of the Creator's handiwork, and they're not to be ignored or despised. Remind your kids, however, that we must always remember to put God's unchanging values *first*. When we do that, we'll have a solid standard that we can apply to the shifting standards of our society. As we'll see in today's session, the Bible provides some implicit guidelines on this topic.

If the kids in your group have grown up in the church, they've heard time and time again the biblical directive to love God with all their

heart, soul, mind, and strength. But only rarely do they apply this commandment to their personal appearance. The problem is that many Christians operate with a mistaken notion that it's possible to separate the "spiritual" matters of the heart from such physical matters as outward appearance. As a result, teens (and adults!) often attempt to live up to God's expectations spiritually while spending a fortune trying to meet their peers' standards for personal appearance.

Of course you know that the Bible is not a guide for good grooming. You won't find the latest fashion trends in its pages (unless robes and sandals make a quick comeback). The Bible does, however, make frequent references to physical appearance. For example, the Bible speaks about hairstyle (Lev. 19:27; 1 Cor. 11:14-15), jewelry (1 Tim. 2:9-10), and clothing (Prov. 31:22; 1 Pet. 3:3). Keep in mind that these passages are descriptive of the culture of their day; they're not necessarily prescriptive for us. Many well-meaning people have missed the point by demanding that Christians should literally follow these biblical descriptions of dress and personal appearance.

It's important to remember that God's claim on our whole being provides the foundation for our discussion about appearances. When we understand that we must love God with both our inner *and* outer appearance, we can begin to consider what will be most pleasing to God. We can also seek to adopt an attitude about personal appearance that puts this concern in its proper perspective.

Hebrews 4:12 gives us a clue in that direction when it tells us that God observes the attitudes of the *heart*. The Lord is interested in pure hearts, to be sure. But he is also interested in how pure hearts come to expression in our personal appearance and in our attitudes toward our appearance.

That's why Christ says: "Why do you worry about clothes? See how the lilies of the field grow. They do not labor or spin. Yet I tell you that not even Solomon in all his splendor was dressed like one of these. . . . Your heavenly Father knows that you need [these things]. But seek first his kingdom and his righteousness" (from Matt. 6:28-34).

Jesus' words speak to the Christian community of all times and places, and set up an ideal against which we all fall short. Our concern about personal appearance needs to be placed in its proper perspective—a task that is not so simple in modern-day North America. But together, as part of the Christian community, we can determine what is appropriate or inappropriate in the way we dress, the makeup we wear, the money we spend on clothing, and the other daily decisions that we make about personal appearance. Taking seriously the Bible's guidelines about modesty and humility, your group should be able to produce guidelines for what is and what is not acceptable.

For Further Study
Following are a few other passages that relate to this issue:

1 Samuel 16:7
Ezekiel 7:15-22
Ezekiel 16:1-19
1 Peter 1:24-25
1 Peter 3:3-4
1 John 2:15-17

MEETING PLAN

1 LOOKIN' GOOD SURVEY
1 5   m i n u t e s

North American society is powerfully influenced by the media. We can see how quickly we are affected by the media when a single song, TV show, or movie becomes "the rage." Hairstyles, dress codes, and the most popular colors are in a constant state of flux as companies promote different products and styles through the media.

Peer group influence is also extremely powerful. Have you been to a mall recently?

Malls are today what fast-food joints and malt shops of the past were to teens. They've become the major gathering places. Kids simply go to the mall to hang out, walk around, talk, and watch each other.

In such an environment, looking good is the main ideal that teens strive for. The pressure to have and wear the latest fashions is extremely strong: if a young person is going to the mall to watch and be watched, he or she certainly doesn't want to look unattractive to his or her peers.

To get your group members thinking along these lines, pass out pencils and Handout 7 ("Lookin' Good Survey"). Without much explanation, ask everyone to work through the handout. Tell them that their answers to the questions are not to be shared with the whole group; instead, they are to be used for self-reflection.

When most or all of the group is finished, ask kids to put their survey answers aside for a few minutes while you reflect together on the whole matter of personal appearance. Distribute Handout 8 ("All the Beautiful People") and ask various group members to read the different sections aloud. This should get your teens thinking about the value of our outward appearance and our inability to attain the "perfect look" that everybody's after.

2 OPINION EXCHANGE
1 5   m i n u t e s

This exercise is intended to help group members understand the difference between *mores*—the way a certain community interprets moral guidelines—and the *morals* behind those interpretations.

Pass Handout 9 ("Which Ones Apply?") to your group members and explain that the items listed are to be placed in two categories: directives that apply to us today and those that apply to a particular time or culture. As they classify these phrases into two groups, ask them to keep track of what they decide by underlining the phrases and biblical directives that apply to us today. *Note:* If you'd like a more visual and communal approach to this exercise, write the sentences on a chalkboard or on newsprint and keep track of the two types yourself.

Follow up with one or two thought-provoking questions, such as the following:

- What do the phrases and passages that you underlined suggest about our personal appearance?

Talk about the fact that Deuteronomy 6:5, Matthew 6:33, and 1 Peter 1:14-19 speak directly to our personal appearance, and the attitude that we need to have about how we look. Our appearance should reflect who we are in Christ.

- What can we learn from the phrases and passages that we didn't underline?

We can still glean important information about attitudes from these other passages. As you discuss this question, try to point participants in the direction of finding some general underlying principals that apply to us today. Talk about the differences in attitudes such as modesty and arrogance, humility and pride. Discuss specifically how a person's excessive concern about how he or she looks stands in direct contrast to the passages discussed in the first question.

3 GUIDELINE BRAINSTORM
15 minutes

In this step you will work with your group members to establish guidelines for personal appearance based on everything you have looked at in the session to this point. Using a fresh sheet of newsprint or your chalkboard, write the heading "Our Guidelines for Personal Appearance."

Open the floor for discussion and accept all of the kids' suggestions with gratitude. In your

discussion, emphasize that we are to love God with our whole being, and that this should be the motivation for the decisions we make about how we look.

In view of last week's budgeting activity, you may want to arrive at some percentage guideline or dollar amount for how much of our income we should be spending on clothing and personal appearance.

After group members brainstorm for about ten minutes, narrow the list down and single out the guidelines that the group feels are most attainable and most applicable to their situation. When you've generated a final list, pass out fresh sheets of paper and pencils and ask everyone to copy the list for their personal reference.

If there is adequate time, refer group members back to the "Lookin' Good Survey." Since they have discussed many different issues in this meeting today, they may have some different attitudes about the responses they wrote down earlier.

4 CLOSING
5 minutes

To close your session today, read Psalm 51:10-12 and Jeremiah 24:7. Let these passages be your transition into a time of prayer. You might want to conclude your meeting with this prayer:

> *Lord, forgive us when we look for meaning, intimacy, and identity not in Christ but in the consumer goods and the unreachable physical standards that this world offers. We recognize that our love is often divided between our own desires and your desires. Help us, Father, to seek your kingdom first. Replace our self-serving hearts with hearts that truly love you. And help us to love you through the way we look, both inside and outside. Amen.*

As the group leaves, give each person a copy of Handout 10 ("Appearance: Getting Beyond the Surface"). Encourage them to use this brief devotional during the week to reinforce the ideas they discussed in this session.

BRAINSTORMING OPTION

If your young people enjoy small group activities, have them split up into groups of three or four to brainstorm guidelines for personal appearance (step 3). Give each small group a sheet of newsprint for keeping their lists. After a few minutes, tape the newsprint pieces to a wall and review them together. Then, on a clean sheet of newsprint, compile a new list under the heading "Our Guidelines for Personal Appearance." Having small groups provide initial guideline ideas may stimulate more creativity when you go over the suggested guidelines as a large group.

CLOSING YOUR SESSION

One effective way of bringing yourself into the closing meditation is to record yourself or someone else reading the Scripture verses and the prayer that you use to close your session. Recording the meditation not only helps young people listen differently, but also shows that you too are a full participant with them and are also in need of prayer.

"THE WARDROBE OF YOUR HEART"

If you have time at the end of today's session, this activity would be a great follow-up to the things your group members have been thinking and talking about in your session. If you use it, let the group know from the beginning that this is a private exercise, and that you'll require complete silence during the activity.

Have the group sit in a circle facing *outward* (be sure to participate in this exercise

yourself). Pass around pieces of scratch paper and ask each person to tear his or her sheet into eight pieces. Have kids close their eyes and sit quietly. Ask them to concentrate on the dots that appear on the backs of their eyelids. Then have them begin to think of words they would use to describe themselves.

After a few minutes, have them open their eyes and write one word on each of the eight pieces of paper. Once they have that done, ask them to arrange the words in order, starting with the most positive and ending with the most negative words.

As they do this, explain to them that each word describes a character trait. These words are like items in a wardrobe, and we wear them like real clothing. Allow the group to meditate on the words, thinking about ways to accentuate the more positive aspects of their personalities.

The aim of this exercise is to give the group an opportunity to express honestly their own feelings about themselves. As your group members sit quietly thinking, make sure that you provide a quiet and calm atmosphere— avoid unnecessary talking.

—Activity adapted from *Human Teaching for Human Learning* by Isaac George Brown. New York: Viking Press, 1971.

Get a Life!

Perhaps when the kids in your group hear the word "steward" they think of a person on a cruise ship who helps passengers with their luggage. Or they might think of flight attendants who serve the needs of airline passengers. Maybe some of the teens in your group would even like to pursue such careers, viewing them as exciting opportunities to travel and meet other people.

That's a great attitude to have when thinking about the idea of being Christian stewards. Even if they're not necessarily thinking of joining the service ranks for their careers, as Christians your teens should be thinking about serving others in God's name. And like the careers mentioned above, the Christian life is filled with wonderful opportunities to serve other people every single day.

Such service to others should not be seen as a boring part of life or as a hassle that depletes a young person's limited resources of time and money. Rather, real Christian stewardship is an exciting way to show Christ's love to others. As we Christians strive to be more like Christ, we can't help but live with stewardly goals in mind.

This concluding meeting, therefore, is designed to help teens think about the future and how they might become better stewards of all their gifts. In the two previous meetings, group members have had opportunities to focus on two specific issues—money and personal appearance. Stewardship, however, extends far beyond those issues. Stewardship is an attitude that pervades a Christian's entire life, finding its outlet through daily actions of service toward others.

- to describe what "stewardship" is and what it implies for daily living
- to distinguish between a self-centered lifestyle and a Christ-centered lifestyle, as taught by the parable of the talents
- to set personal stewardship goals for the future in line with what we discussed in this course

1. Bibles
2. Pens/pencils
3. Handouts 11-13 and Evaluation Form
4. Scratch paper
5. Several aprons or large cloth pieces to cover clothes
6. Blindfolds
7. Several bowls and spoons
8. Different foods such as applesauce, pudding, Jell-O, and the like

The main scriptural focus of this session is Matthew 25:14-30, commonly referred to as the parable of the talents. In this passage Jesus tells the story of a rich man who, before leaving on a trip, decides to put his servants to work while he's gone. The rich man gives ten talents to one servant, five to another, and one to still another. After being gone for some time, the master returns and asks his servants to report on their progress. He's greatly pleased that the first two servants have put the funds entrusted to them to work and have gained a return on their investment. But the rich man is extremely displeased with the third servant, who neglected to put the master's money at risk and instead buried it in the ground. This third servant is reprimanded and punished for his inactivity.

This story in Matthew stands in the context of two other stories about the end times. The parable of the ten virgins, the parable of the talents, and the parable of the sheep and the goats all deal with the coming time of judgment and how we are to prepare for Christ's return. Luke 19 says specifically that Jesus told this parable because some people thought that "the kingdom of God was going to appear at once." Evidently the parable of the talents is meant to point out that there will be a considerable period of time when the king is gone and we need to do our work. At the end of that time the king will return and call us to account for what we've done or haven't done in the service of the kingdom.

The kids in your group may feel that the treatment the third servant received was unfair. After all, wasn't he doing the safe thing? What if he had risked his money and lost? They may see his conservative action as commendable, not as something that warrants punishment.

But look at the story from the master's point of view. Having hired these three servants for the betterment of his estate, he expected them to get busy and work with the money he had given them. How would any of your group members' employers feel about them if they punched in on the time clock and then sat down in the break room for fear of risking life and limb flipping burgers?

The master's action was a pure business proposition. Even if the third servant had tried and failed to make more money, he would have at least been commended for taking a risk for the benefit of his master's estate. This servant's attitude was really self-serving; by burying the money he was basically just trying to cover himself so that he wouldn't be punished when the owner returned.

The question of risk is an important one. The third servant's excuse for not taking a risk is the accusation that the master is a hard man who is very demanding of his servants. That excuse is balanced with the other two servants

acting in faithful service. In the end the master commends those who are faithful in serving him, even during his absence.

In applying the teachings of this parable, structure your discussion so that it centers around the question of who we are really serving in this world—ourselves or God? The third servant didn't have the best interests of his master in mind. Do we have the best interests of God and his kingdom in mind? Are we willing to risk the resources and abilities we've been given for the betterment of God's kingdom?

Let your group members know that serving others doesn't necessarily mean committing themselves to a lifetime of mission work and living in a dirt-floored hut in some faraway country. While a career of full-time Christian service is commendable and should be seriously considered, such service is not necessarily for everyone. Most importantly, you need to emphasize that living as a Christian *is* a full-time service occupation, no matter what career path your teens choose.

Whatever their goals for the future, encourage the kids in your group to develop a Christlike attitude of service to others. Jesus' whole purpose on earth was to serve humanity. He did this in small ways, such as when he took the time to bless little children; but he also performed the ultimate act of service to humanity when he took on all of our sin. Remind your group that a life lived in imitation of Christ requires an attitude of service that colors all of our perception.

For Further Study
Other passages that you might refer to on this issue include the following:

Matthew 22:37; 23:5-7, 11-12, 23-27
Ephesians 2:10
Philippians 2:3-8

1 FEEDING FRENZY

15 minutes

Start this final meeting out with a bang as you prepare to look at the attitudes of Christian stewardship and servanthood.

To begin this fun and sloppy group exercise, have the kids pair off. Tell them that you are going to be acting out the theme of this session—servanthood and stewardship—and that, in addition, you'll all get something to eat!

Directions:
1. Situate the kids in a semicircle with one chair in the middle. Place a large cloth underneath the chair.
2. Ask for the first volunteer pair to move to the center, with one of the kids sitting down and the other standing behind the chair.
3. Ask the person sitting down what he or she would like to eat from among your choices. Then place a blindfold and an apron on that person.
4. Place the food in a bowl and set it on the seated person's lap. Then ask the seated person to sit on his or her hands—the use of hands is not allowed in this exercise.
5. Blindfold the individual behind the chair, and instruct that person to feed his or her partner from the bowl.
6. Have fun!

After all who want to participate have had a turn, clean up and then discuss a couple of questions:

- Who was the servant in this activity?
- What does this activity have to do with stewardship?

On the one hand, group members could see the feeding as an act of "service" to another person (even though it may have caused a mess and wasn't necessarily appreciated!).

Stewardship involves using our resources or abilities in helping others in some way.

On the other hand, they may see this activity in a negative light. Sometimes we waste our resources and do a poor job of being stewards in God's kingdom. You might ask the group to mention times when we tend to waste our resources and abilities. Good stewardship involves careful and effective use of our resources and abilities.

2 GROUP DISCUSSION

20 minutes

For your discussion today, you'll be taking a close look at the parable of the talents (Matt. 25:14-30). But tell the kids that you'll want to place a different twist on this discussion: Rather than you as leader asking standard questions, group members will be developing their own questions as they read the passage.

Pass out copies of Handout 11 ("The Parable of the Talents") to the group. Then give them ten minutes to go through the entire parable and jot down their ideas for the categories of questions listed on the back of the page. Each person should write his or her own questions.

Once everyone has completed this task, ask different individuals to volunteer one of their questions in each category. Again, look for attitudes that indicate that God expects us to invest all that he gives us to build the kingdom. The information in this meeting's Theme Thoughts should help you direct the discussion.

As you examine the parable of the talents together, consider *why* the third servant acted the way he did. Was it out of fear? Did he not trust himself to make decisions about things that did not belong to him? Or did he simply not see himself as part of his master's plan?

Once you have considered the attitudes of the third servant, turn the discussion around and ask the same questions of the first two servants. How did their attitudes differ from the third servant? And don't forget to look at the end result of the three servants' actions—not in a threatening way, but rather as a positive way to encourage the kids in your group to consciously consider their work for God in the world around them.

Once you feel you've worked through the parable and drawn some applicable conclusions about stewardship from the story, move on to the next step of this session.

3 LOOKING BACK, LOOKING AHEAD

15 minutes

Comment that "stewardship" is an attitude that touches every part of our lives: our needs and wants, how we handle our money, how we present ourselves to others, and so on.

Encourage your group members to consider setting goals for their lives based on the things they've learned in the course. Pass a copy of Handout 12 ("Looking Back, Looking Ahead") to everyone, challenging each person in your group to read through it and to set personal goals based on the review information.

When most of the group have finished, invite them to share one or more goals with a partner. You can give a certain amount of "accountability" to the goal-setting if the partners check back with each other during your next meeting. You can also invite the partners to pray for each other during the week.

4 CLOSING THE MEETING

5 minutes

Pass out the "Evaluation Form" and ask the kids to complete it. There's also an evaluation form for you to fill out at the end of this leader's guide. We would appreciate your efforts in completing the evaluation so that we can better serve your needs in the future.

After the kids have finished their evaluations, conclude this course of study by suggesting that your group members spend a minute in silent prayer, reflecting on the goals they outlined for themselves in the previous step. Conclude the prayer yourself, asking the Spirit to encourage each person to fulfill his or her goals and to live a truly Christ-centered lifestyle.

OPTIONS

HANDOUT 13 ("THE GUY WHO WANTED A LITTLE BIT OF EVERYTHING")

This fictional story helps build an understanding of God's priorities for teens' lives. It encourages them to realize that being a Christian—and being a servant—requires 100 percent commitment. If you'd like, you could substitute this story for the warm-up activity in step 1.

IDEAS FOR SERVING

A perfect way to nail down the ideas about stewardship that you've discussed in this session would be to have your group members work together on a stewardship project. Habitat for Humanity and places like your local soup kitchen and local mission organizations are always looking for eager young individuals to help them along in their ministry. Check your phone book for numbers and locations of local service organizations.

If you'd rather use your kids' abilities and energy in your own congregation, ask your pastor if anyone in your congregation could use some help—whether that be painting, yard work, or a trip to the grocery store. Such activities would help the members of your congregation to better communicate with the teens in your group, and could foster good, long-term relationships of service.

If you need another meeting to coordinate a service project, by all means make the time to do so. What's more, you should give the responsibility for planning and coordinating the project over to the group. Doing so will give the kids a sense of ownership for the project and may motivate them to take the lead in future service projects. Above all, encourage them to have fun with whatever project they undertake. Working for the Lord is a privilege, and God is the most loving employer in the universe!

G O T T A   H A V E   I T !

Leader Evaluation Form

BACKGROUND

Size of group:
- [ ] under 5
- [ ] 5-9
- [ ] 10-15
- [ ] over 15

School grade of participants:
- [ ] grade 10
- [ ] grade 11
- [ ] grade 12
- [ ] post-high

Length of group sessions:
- [ ] under 30 minutes
- [ ] 30-45 minutes
- [ ] 45-60 minutes
- [ ] over 60 minutes

Please check items that describe you:
- [ ] male
- [ ] female
- [ ] ordained or professional church staff
- [ ] elder or deacon
- [ ] professional teacher
- [ ] church school or catechism teacher (three or more years)
- [ ] youth group leader

HANDOUTS FOR GROUP MEMBERS

In general, I
- [ ] did not use the handouts
- [ ] used the handouts frequently

Please check items that describe the handouts:
- [ ] too few
- [ ] too many
- [ ] helpful
- [ ] not helpful

LEADER'S GUIDE AND GROUP PROCESS

Please check items that describe the activities suggested for each group session:
- [ ] varied
- [ ] monotonous
- [ ] creative
- [ ] dull
- [ ] clear
- [ ] unclear
- [ ] interesting to participants
- [ ] uninteresting to participants
- [ ] too many
- [ ] too few

Please check the items that describe the Theme Thoughts provided in the leader's guide:
- [ ] helpful, stimulating
- [ ] not helpful or stimulating
- [ ] overly complex, long
- [ ] about right level of difficulty
- [ ] clear
- [ ] unclear

The course in general was true to the Reformed/Presbyterian tradition.
- [ ] agree
- [ ] disagree
- [ ] not sure

Please check those procedures that worked best for you:
- [ ] games
- [ ] small group activities and discussion
- [ ] whole group activities and discussion
- [ ] handouts
- [ ] session options
- [ ] other (please write in)

_____
_____
_____

Please check the items that describe the group sessions:

☐ lively
☐ dull
☐ dominated by leader
☐ involved most participants
☐ relevant to lives of participants
☐ irrelevant to lives of participants
☐ worthwhile
☐ not worthwhile

In general I would rate this material as

☐ excellent
☐ good
☐ fair
☐ poor

Additional comments on any aspect of this program:

_____

Name (optional)

_____

Church

_____

City/State/Province

Please send completed form to:

LifeWise
CRC Publications
2850 Kalamazoo Ave. SE
Grand Rapids, Michigan 49560

Thank you!